NEVER NIGHT

poems

DERICK BURLESON

MARICK PRESS

LIBRARY OF CONGRESS CATALOGUING IN PUBLICATION DATA

Burleson, Derick
Never Night.
Poems in English

ISBN: 978-0-9712676-5-7

Copyright © by Derick Burleson, 2007
Edited by Ilya Kaminsky
Design and typesetting by Sean Tai
Cover design by Sean Tai

Cover image: *West Ridge October*, © Kesler Woodward, 2006. One of Alaska's best known artists, Kesler Woodward has painted the landscape of the circumpolar North for three decades, from Hudson Bay in Arctic Canada to Russia's Siberian coast.

Printed and bound in Canada

Marick Press
P.O. Box 36253
Grosse Pointe Farms
Michigan 48236
www.marickpress.com

Distributed by spdbooks.org

for Nicole and Mirabel Keats Sprague Burleson

ACKNOWLEDGEMENTS

Grateful acknowledgments to the editors of the following journals in which these poems first appeared:

Alaska Quarterly Review: "New House on Narrowview Lane."
Gulf Coast: "Prophet."
Fox Cry Review: "After the Battle," "Alabaster Caverns."
Kansas Quarterly/Arkansas Review: "Turbulence."
lyric: "Outside Fairbanks," "Enterprise," "Late Valentine."
The National Poetry Review: "Late Valentines," "Spring Fall."
Neo: "Garden," "Hour," "Migration," "Some Names."
Petroglyph: "From Montana with Love."
Poetry: "Never Night," "After This," "Skipping School."
Poetry Northwest: "Catastrophe on Sixth Street."
Sage Magazine: "Omega Bend," "Two Headed Moose Fetus Found Near Clear."
Seattle Review: "Persephone."
The Southern Review: "American Boys," "Harvest," "In Our Field."
Western Humanities Review: "News From Here," "Roadwork," "North Jetty."

I would like to thank the National Endowment for the Arts for a fellowship that supported the writing of these poems. Many thanks to my colleagues and students at the University of Alaska–Fairbanks, and to my friends and teachers for their endless support and help with these poems, especially: Gerri Brightwell, Anne Caston, David

Conway, Sarah Doetschman, Mark Doty, Eugene Gloria, Patricia Goedicke, Al Gee, Cindy Hardy, Sean Hill, Edward Hirsch, Jonathan Holden, Richard Howard, Anne-Corrine Kell, Mike Koskey, Anita Leverich, Alex Lewandowski, John Morgan, Greg Pape, Kate Quick, Barbara Ras, John Reinhard, Steve Rubenstein, Peggy Shumaker, Ed Skoog, Frank Soos, Amber Flora Thomas, Kesler Woodward, Jean Valentine, Robert Wrigley and Adam Zagajewski. I am very grateful to Ilya Kaminsky for selecting and editing this book, and to Mariela Griffor and Marick Press for publishing it.

TABLE OF CONTENTS

3. LATE VALENTINES

1. American Boys

Think of the long trip home.

IN OUR FIELD

The sun and dust and wind and straw and wheat
stubble and me and a tractor howling
before the plow, and my dead grandfather
drifting over my shoulder, whispering,
whispering all through that long July,
tracing the same furrow he followed
half a century ago trudging behind four horses.
Gulls and egrets soar the shrinking squares
we plow, spinning long days of red dust
into always. Why have they come? For every
blinking toad the plow turns up, blind and dazed
by the white shock of sun, eaten before it burrows
back down into cool earth. Our field that summer
was the absence of absence, peopled by the local gods
of history: a jackrabbit bursts from the tumbleweeds
bordering the railroad right-of-way. What makes
that rabbit run so madly through afternoon heat shimmers?
The coyote hungry enough to hunt this time
of day, hungry enough to carve circles
across the fresh-plowed field for an hour until they collapse,
until the coyote crawls forward to end the rabbit's history.
I didn't know what to wish for. A field of my own?
Reason enough to endure the heat and howl of endless
rounds in the field among the gulls and all the dead
cutting perfect furrows behind ghost horses,
and we danced the stubble field round and round
until the moon came up and the sun went down.

GARDEN

I am in the garden on hands and knees
because I can't walk yet. I remember
the smell, how my hands disappear when I press
first one then the other down into the earth,
the smell of fresh-turned loam like a forethought
of death. I am already halfway home
there in the garden where I remember
this first memory, a seed that might grow.
My mother plants a row of green onions,
though I don't know onion from any other
plant there in the garden where I don't know
potato from tomato, where it seems
I am not my mother, but me disappearing
bit by bit into the loam from which I sprang,
a green bean uncoiling from the bean seed
Mother will plant when she finishes the row
of onions. I only remember the smell
of loam, how my hands vanished, and the sun.
I felt the sun hot on my bald head inside
of which a green bean was right then springing
forth, head seething in heat, hands, vanishing.

SKIPPING SCHOOL

And then it rained days and nights at a time,
rained until the rising water swept through
our house like spring cleaning and carried

my bed and me still in it away down the raging
river that used to be Main Street. I can still see
my mother with a healthy glass of orange juice,

standing on the porch, near where the door was
before Main Street ran through my room.
The bed began to spin and rainwater foamed

all around, railroad tracks turned to rapids
and all the stop signs swept away. My bed
rose and fell, bucking half-hearted like a green-

broke colt. I was wide-eyed, not at the ride,
but at the households loose in that flood,
a whole Main street awash in dirty laundry,

the next-door neighbors' Brittany spaniel still
chained, howling on top of its house, even
a man who must have been my father just

sitting down to lunch at the floating kitchen table,
one eye still on the television weather.
I dreamed that Main Street wound on

forever, through all the wheat fields,
past small-town grain elevators gleaming
in the distance like bright ivory towers.

Then the river widened into interstate and all
the other kids who'd skipped school began to build
bed-slat masts and raise bed-sheet sails and the wind

always blew from the right direction
as we sailed on together through neon cities
we'd never heard of, then out across the bay,

over the chaos of the ocean until we struck
land far from home, found the horses tethered,
patient as a promise.

ALABASTER CAVERNS

Our guide is a goddess
dressed all in olive and I'm in love.
She leads us down into the cave mouth.

It's the end of 7th Grade, early May.
We pull on windbreakers, sniffing
guano, condensation glinting

beneath ranks of bare bulbs.
Her flashlight points out stalactites,
cascades of limestone, marl chutes

still flowing down to depths
spelunkers have yet to penetrate.
She illuminates a chimney writhing

with bats, albino catfish in the creek.
Look close – these fish have no eyes.
We descend into the widest chamber

and she herds us together,
plays her flashlight around
the corners: sunshine yellow canisters

full of soda crackers and hard candy
in case of nuclear war. We'll be safe
for years from radioactive fallout.

There's only one small hitch.
She turns and flicks a hidden
switch, commanding the world

to go out. Now this is total dark.
I stumble back a step, the night
so night it feels like drowning

feels in dreams, a whirlpool
taking me down by the ankles.
Is love this blind? A night

filtered pure through
the filaments of pin oak roots?
Then it's light again when

the underworld comes back
on with a snap. She gives us a wink.
I stare back and she blurs through my tears.

AMERICAN BOYS

The salt is flame in his eyes,
and he doesn't know how or why
the mud fight has turned and now
they circle around
and fling fistfuls of mud and sand
at him who has done them no wrong.

You wouldn't want to swim
in the Great Salt Plains Lake
but they do, since it's the only lake
near their one stoplight
town and this is late spring.

They are Cub Scouts, wading out
into thick red Oklahoma mud,
and salty water. The salt in his eyes
stings, and they surround
him like turkey buzzards
circling fresh road-killed meat.

Like bluebottle flies around shit.
The sky burns white and blue.
Why have they chosen him,
a bookish boy on the football team?
He breaks through the circle
and wades back to shore.

He'd kill them – kill them all if he could.
The salt stings his eyes;

his eyes burn from mud.
I know because he is me,
or was. I hated them then –

still do. That day, though,
I would have traded places
with anyone – with anyone.
Even one of them.

HARVEST

He stands beside his father on the Gleaner
gripping the metal rail tight in both hands
staring down into the sun blur of sickle,
clouds of dust and straw and chaff blown behind,
and all the way to the horizon, to the curve
of round earth across the plain, nothing but wheat
and a cloud of dust for each combine cutting.
When wheat fills the machine, his father starts
the auger and a stream of gold pours into
the truck, where he is not allowed to play
since nearly every year a boy falls asleep
in the sun on that pile of gold smelling
of bread in the heat of late June and is
buried alive by his father under
the grain we in those parts of Oklahoma
all lived to raise from red soil. Thirteen hours
the sun spun across unbroken blue sky,
thirteen hours we and the Gleaner gleaned
until moon rose and dew fell too heavy
down and wet the ripe wheat, and the silence
in that absence of machine was an abyss
only crickets could understand. I see the boy
there on that machine, the sure hands of his father
on the wheel, on the levers that sped or
slowed, raised or lowered to keep the wheat feeding
evenly in. How the boy stares down into
that spin of bright hot steel, of well-oiled blade
against steel cutter bar, the auger whirling,
a steel cylinder pulling fate and will together

where steel fingers grab grain and chaff and straw,
shove it all into the metal monster's
ravenous maw. I watch the boy hold tight
and I hope he will not fall.

TURBULENCE

If you could see it when
the Medicine River goes crazy
every early spring and begins
to boil all red and muddy,
rolling the rain down
across the Kansas border,
you might imagine, like I do,
something secret surging under

the turbid surface, maybe
catfish big enough to eat you,
until someone older, say a grandfather
explains how the current can suck you down.
Even grown men drown trying to swim
when the river's like that, he says.

Through the dusty windows
of an abandoned church on the edge
of a prairie where no man and no farm wife
and not even the children
have attended in thirty years
you can see how some slow pull
still twists the summer sun
until evening sweeps away

the withered windbreak elms outside,
making such faith seem an easy choice.
But if you still don't believe glass

is a slow liquid, no one will stop you
from breaking out each pane to see
how much settles to the bottom.

NORTH JETTY

Spy satellite sees a blue circle bisected
by a fine pink line, and zooming closer, two black points
polluting the purity of the line:

That's me and David. For us, the sea is divided,
neat as if Aaron laid down Moses' staff
between gulf and bay. Granite monoliths

tilted, strewn every which way, held up
by sharp-edged riprap and nothing.
A bad fall would be fatal.

It's a good thing
we're already damned.
We've been damned a long time now,

long enough to memorize
each particular pattern of pink feldspar,
hornblende, and white quartz earth-heat

and earth-push metamorphosed once
into these rough hewn cubes
civilization could build a pyramid of.

We clamber over, clamber
north toward a terra firma
which erodes, recedes with each wave,

with each summer's heavy hurricane.
David's gone on ahead, and who can blame him?
At this distance, a tiny stick man

weighing down a fine line boundaried
by most of the planet's salt.
My two bad knees stumble on,

sun startling water from flesh,
calcium from bone,
coagulating capillary blood.

The ocean's full of man o' wars
and blue crabs and stingrays, claws
and stingers poised, feeding on the carrion

of each other. A lone glaucous gull squawks
overhead, prophesying nothing
but more algae-slimed rock to cross

and the west wind shreds high tide,
lashes my left side with salt-sand spray.
The water smells of death and gasoline.

We're already dead.
We've been dead a long time now.
Even if we fall we'll be reborn into this:

shrimp trawlers crawl in trailing empty
sun-rotted nets like the wings of ragged butterflies
nearing the end of their annual migrations.

There are no shrimp.
There have been no shrimp forever.
Oil still pours a rainbow

from its corroded barge. Hasn't it always
been flowing? Hasn't our blood? Out of reach
a dolphin blows, breathes, sinks.

ROADWORK

One worker and one bulldozer are eating every street in the city.
What they don't get the floods do. Cars slow past the barriers,
speed up on the other side. The flood washes fire ants out of their mounds.

It's dangerous living like this. Where are the trucks to haul away the rubble?
Where are the other workers? When will they rebuild the streets?
All night the yellow flashing lights of the warning barrels dance.

Will I make it to work on time? What if the wheel comes off?
They never summon the workers to rebuild the streets.
Sometimes when I'm doing eighty I pass right between

twin eighteen-wheelers. I wonder if the worker and the bulldozer get lonely
eating the streets. What do they say to each other when things go wrong?
When the asphalt crumbles instead of breaking into neat chunks? When it

clouds up and rains and keeps on raining? Sometimes the warning beacons
seem confusing. Should I merge left or right to reach the airport on time?
Sometimes fish eat the fire ants and die from the fire in their bellies.

It's dangerous living like this. It doesn't always flood. Sometimes it's sunny
for weeks on end. They never summon work crews to clear away the rubble.
Grackles love the carrion that washes up when it floods.

CATASTROPHE ON SIXTH

At the core of the day, a demolition
derby driver fresh back from the derby
in Plains tried to pass me on the left
while I was changing lanes, crumpled
my pickup door like the skulls
long-dead Samson crushed with the jawbone

of an ass. While Montana spiraled through
its arm of the Milky Way, the few Pabst
Blue Ribbons I had not already drunk
that Sunday afternoon silently turned
to foam on the passenger's side, cold
under steel caps. My parents confessed

not long ago I was a child unprepared for,
an after-church mistake on the '62 Ford's
back seat, the egg accepting one among
spiral galaxies of sperm. While black
holes gnawed through any belts of matter
they could find, funneling energy

through time like water under Hoover Dam,
Skoog sauntered down from his upstairs
apartment to see what all the racket
was about. Quarks crashed through his nuclei,
but he didn't seem to mind. The demolition
derby driver's boot abused his well used

Chevy, the crumpled steel fender of which
must have felt happy to know it was headed
for the crusher. The rest of the universe
expanded toward one more agonized contraction,
and in the nexus of nearly-fused hydrogen,
new stars birthed new constellations.

This is why we buy insurance: the late sun
surely was in everybody's eyes that day.
Skoog and I went fishing anyway, opened
and sipped foamy beers, cast to rainbow trout
that couldn't resist rising while molten yellow
leaves struggled a bit, then hissed into the river.

FROM MONTANA WITH LOVE

I'm sending this out in a plain manila package.
I've licked each stamp myself.

From our proud mountain ranges, Rattlesnakes, Missions and Crazies
I'm sending you one spruce box, intricately carved, full of some
of what we have this side of the continental divide:

miners leaching gold from ore with bitter-almond cyanide,
loggers logging third-growth Ponderosa forests and stands
of slim larch, smelters, steakhouses, pulp mills, glossy pamphlets

full of anglers cradling rainbow trout whose cartilaginous skulls
even now discern the first ticklings of a disease that in a few weeks
will leave them chasing their tails across those companionable streams

Lewis and Clark and Sacagawea waded west. I'm sending you
bighorns and pronghorns, the sawn-off antlers of whitetails,
moose and elk, a breeding pack of reintroduced Yellowstone wolves,

the pelt of the last grizzly ever to rummage a dumpster.
I'm sending a glacier, a ski lift, cirques and peaks, no-speed-limit
highways, four lanes crowded with RVs whizzing past ranches,

home to the strong men and women who each year vaccinate
vast herds of Herefords, who eat blizzards with milk
for breakfast, who believe in justice and the Constitution

with all their hearts, whose ancestors laid the steel tracks
where derailed tank-cars belch clouds of enough chlorine
to purify every swimming pool west of the Mississippi.

Well go on. Open it.
Open it.

ENTERPRISE

When in the chronicle of wasted time
I consider how much TV I watch –
five generations of Star Trek – my rhyme
goes slant. For what can compare with that box
of pixels stacked on pixels and its pure
radiations? Spock the logical one
with pointy ears, Kirk the man of action,
and the Enterprise herself, more power
with each new season. We live for narrative.
When night falls every window turns bright blue.
Phasers fire, and I come full alive
in the continuing quest for what is true
and alien. Form warps the whole argument
when I consider how my light is spent.

OMEGA BEND

Here's where the world comes to an end.
Floods all spring and the snagged roots
of what was once a yellow pine growing
too close to the river. Only now
the river has gone back to its banks,
now the river has gone back to its banks
and sun wants you to believe it's July.
If the river snatched the silver star
I've worn for years now, snatched the star
when my body fell back into clear water
thawed from Bitterroot snow, whose sin was that?
I hope a boulder wears it now, that star,
or that it washes up on the beach of fine
sand glittering alive with flecks of mica.
The children still wet from the river
rolled themselves in hot sand that afternoon
as in powdered sugar or powdered gold
and flung it into the sun all afternoon
in bright streamers of joy: the river sand,
the sun wanted to eat us all with joy
that day where rattlesnakes slither through star-
thistle, where red-tailed hawks snatch those
diamondbacks and teach them to fly, where ospreys
snatch rainbow trout and teach them to fly,
where every morning wind blows upstream
and evening blows down, where that afternoon
truly loved the gold of wheat fields, the gold
pastures of cheat grass and sweet grass growing
through the pumice of an ancient volcano where

the sharpest possible sliver of the new moon
sliced over the deck of this house built safe
far above the Clearwater River on a cliff
and the wind in my face felt like sea wind
as on the deck of a ship on which
someday we will sail down this river
all the way to the Pacific to watch
the stars at the end of the world go out.

AFTER THIS

We'll all walk together
out of this room, through
that door, down the worn

stairs and out into the twilight.
No matter what else happens,
we'll kick through fallen leaves

to hear the sounds they make
like all kinds of water running together.
And when our talk fades, when music

is only music again, we will slowly dim,
just our eyes and the teeth of our shy smiles
still showing. We'll go back

to our own places and finally sleep,
smug with the fierce pleasure
of knowing that soul is the particular

song we learn to sing, that our lovers
will always be gardens beside us,
blooming the colors we dream best,

graceful as the glittering waves,
bursting on a moonlit beach
beyond the foot of our beds.

2. North

Should we have stayed at home and thought of here?

NEVER NIGHT

You'd like it here where
it's never night, where the sun
circles, rather, until it ends
up where it started from,
east or west, rises, sinks
but doesn't ever set,
where in the summer
you never need to sleep
and all day and all night
the sky is a series of blues
you've seen only once before,
blues van Gogh painted
at the end. Where all the traffic
is fox and moose and bear,
where aspen and birch
bud and leaf all in one day,
and your sleep, when sleep
finally comes, is innocent,
spring wind through a window
left open now that spring
is passing fast and summer
won't stay here long before
the snow sweeps any green
away again and then it's always
night. You'd like that too, when
endless night falls and the moon
comes up, reads your book over
your shoulder, learns which dead

poet moves you tonight,
when any heat at all rises,
and becomes a visible thing.

HOUR

Now the hour badly spent has passed,
I sit outside in late September sun,
book in hand, the season passing fast,

faster than I've ever seen. Leaves
(aspen? birch? I don't know which.
It's hard to tell from here) flame to yellow

while I watch, then fall. I can hear
the construction workers shouting
at the yellow crane to lift it higher,

higher. One worker swabs the roof
with a mop full of tar. Beside me
in the sun, a swallow, I think. I pick it up

to be sure, only feathers left, a little skin,
its eyeless head. Did it smash into the window?
My office window up above? Spring's nests

clung there until (What did I read?)
the workers washed them down last week.
All the living swallows winged it south by now.

OUTSIDE FAIRBANKS

Mist this morning rises up
the valley like a nightmare
fading toward noon, until

I can't remember what
the horror was, rises from
the poison pond the gold

mine left, gilds the golden
aspen leaves with acid dew.
Late fall and the chickadees

already brave enough to eat
sunflower seeds from my hand.
A semi rumbles down Gold

Hill Road below, hauling who
knows what hazard toward town
while wild cranberries fill

the gelid air with a foretaste
of winter scent. Such strange
juxtapositions. And I wonder

what gasses my oil stove breathes
out, keeping me close and cozy
while the cold season rises.

I stood alone and watched
the northern lights last night,
a goddess lashing her moon-

bearing horses home late
with a sharp whip of green
flame. Now the morning

mist has risen here, turned
to a blank fog the far sun
can't break through.

SPRING FALL

When the Monitor heater quit heating
I figured it had run out of diesel.

Early April, still plenty of snow
around, but the frozen ground

already softer than you'd think.
The fuel tank on its scaffold had tilted,

though I didn't know that yet. I remember
the gunshot in the Oasis Cafe that night,

the skid, which could have spun out otherwise,
but didn't. I've been spinning for years

now through an instant the bomb
went off in the bar we were walking to,

killing some I might have known
but didn't. Now all seems well

here in the Alaskan interior. I'm out of fuel,
that's all. Birches turn toward the sun

and bask, plan to leaf out soon. On the second
rung, I reach for the fuel tank cap. How

has the stove burned 300 gallons of diesel so
soon? Something's shifting. Sun renders

the scaffold rickety and weaker. Longer
days, more sun and brighter. Earth melts, I learn,

beneath cruel April snow. I reach. No time
to think, to spin away from what danger

would come, no time to miss my wife or
revise my life. I reach towards toward.

That little tilt rocks the fuel tank's cradle,
and down will fall fuel tank, Derick and all.

"TWO-HEADED MOOSE FETUS FOUND NEAR CLEAR"

We believe there is no
or very little evidence
linking this discovery

to the top secret military
radar listening post
installation near Clear,

and furthermore that
the people of Clear
have absolutely nothing,

or little, to fear.
It's just an impossibility.
There are hazards,

of course, but you have
to be right there,
practically kissing

the radar face to be
in any danger
whatsoever. Of course

we'll be conducting
an intense investigation
including X-rays, dissection

and genetic screening,
all that good science,
but as of this moment

in time we firmly
believe that this incident
has absolutely no

or little relevance to
the issue at hand.
We wish to assure

you that to us
the public health
is of the absolute

utmost importance,
and the people living
near Clear, including

those who ate the cow
moose have nothing,
or little, to fear.

PROPHET

When snow falls thick
among bare aspens,
I will wade down into

this vale and begin
to make my soul.
When midnight dawns

frozen with no moon
to silver the night,
I will begin with words

made visible, frozen
words rising on no
wind among the black

blind eyes of bare aspen,
rising into midnight
sky with none to hear

except sleeping ravens,
and the world will grow
rife with strange green fire.

SOME NAMES

Aspen leaves falling fast
drift against the cabin door,
carpet the forest floor, fill
below zero air with the traffic

of leaves and the absence
of leaves. Yes, wind tonight
and the bare trees white like
the exposed bones of a land's

forgotten dead, bones eroded
into moonlight. If poets were
exiled here, they'd hear the pure
click of aspen. Wind tonight,

bare trees, and all the golden
leaves spiral down. Death
alone can stop the fall, hold
aspen leaves tight to aspen trees.

MIGRATION

When Sandhill cranes arrive delivering news
from the Realm of Warm in gurgling cries

we can't understand, we sing spring is here.
Cranes fly from summer back to summer,

dragging the sun behind elegant outstretched legs.
And when the river turns liquid again, they land

here where carnivores welcome the annual feast
of eggs transformed to flesh in the secret

alchemy of nests. Cranes never need to learn
winter's bleak, creaking words and weave slow

wing beats into a sad song of transience.
Birch trees scribble this tale of departure

in yellow flame. We name it September and burn
the birch to warm our homes, yearning

for hollow bones and a journey south toward
new lands and a stronger slant of sun.

NEWS FROM HERE

The news from here this morning
is frost rimed trees and frost
falling in light breeze, making

zero seem colder than it is. Who?
Me, and the steady hiss inside
my skull, saying nothing,

nothing, except listen. When?
Sunrise later every morning
than the last, until it's noon

before the sun orange flame
rings frost to life. Where?
Arctic, north of sun's realm,

silent except for the hiss
of frost falling in what sun
there is and breeze. How?

I'm not sure. These aspen
trees belong to moose
and snowshoe hare and fox,

chickadees beginning now
to flit from spruce to spruce.
What news there is the raven

knows and calls it loud, making
quiet seem more quiet after. How?
Snow has fallen, snow will fall,

below zero riming trees
with frost until they wear
sparkling fur on every bare

branch. That voice, that voice,
a static hiss of frost this morning,
the hiss of northern lights last night,

and full moon, the harvest moon,
though harvest is long past here.
Where? Here, Love, I'm here,

alone and silent, red moon
rising, rising white until
night seems no longer night.

3. Late Valentines

Where should we be today?

LATE VALENTINES

I.

My darling, I have imagined you dead,
or worse, dying in my arms, a tragic
victim of the gods' cataclysmic magic,
the eternal scissors grazing your thread

with an icy misstep and a long fall
or the city chimneys' subtle poison,
or a murderer paroled from prison,
secondhand smoke, a stray shard of shrapnel.

And so tonight I touch your face and pray
the three sisters will kill us together,
fusing our molecules into one slow dance,

in death as in breath, cold choice and hot chance
tuning our voices to the tornadic weather
it takes to love long and perish each day.

II.

Today on our walk you turned your ankle.
And that was no small thing, the pain you felt,
clouds across the sun, a shadow to foretell
storms of pain to come. Oh, the acute angles

our bodies make in love, elbow and knee,
rib and hip, shoulder blade and collarbone.

How can I forgive that numb, random stone,
the years, (if we survive), those aches we'll feel?

If this were the last rhyme I ever write,
what should my hands choose to fabricate?
They'd spin straw into gold to bribe the fates,
stitch a bright charm against the sprain of night,

and weave one last tapestry of our tears,
so we can ache another ten thousand years.

III.

The week you turned thirty-five your father
died, and I can think of no easy way
to say that: He went to sleep and never
woke up. What was he dreaming? Now today

it's your birthday. I wanted to build you
a white house with a green picket fence. I
wanted to build a trellis and bring you
a fresh rose. I wanted to give you – I

wanted to say that your father is still
dreaming, that heaven is whatever we dream
when we sleep in the house, which has and will
continue to settle into what we become.

I wanted to give you not was but is.
Love, all I could build to give you is this.

AFTER THE BATTLE

The world returns.
Hilltops emerge
like green dreams

from muddy water
and trees toss
new leaves. The couple

sends out a bird –
who cares what
color. It flies back

with muddy feet,
then away again
to the first island.

They fall to their knees,
thank the bird,
and then pray,

two faint voices
winging over infinite
water to where a god

bakes a world fresh
each day, clouds
and sun and wind,

dancing the steps
of making. A nod
of the famous head,

a word, and water
and fire unite with
the same fertile

discord that first set
the world singing.
And the boulders

strewn in war,
articulate fragments
of the mountains

they heaved in rage,
become men and women
again, who love

each other in the mute
struggle to escape
their granite flesh.

PERSEPHONE

My mistress' bright eyes are near-sighted
and more green sea than earth some days
given her mood and the weather. She won't wear
her glasses, silly girl, and so must squint
to see far away. I've seen her squint to see
far away before, but she didn't say
what she saw. I'm a blur to her which is what
maybe, she loves, never close enough to see,
or to smell the breath that reeks from me. Once,
twice we hugged, but we never kissed.
I guess she isn't really my mistress.
Yet I love her bookish ways. She'd rather
kiss Sartre and all her dead romantic darlings.
Her eyes can see into the deep heart of things.
Her legs are strong enough for climbing me,
her ankles thick as young aspens, as dancers'.
She has tea and cigarettes for breakfast.
When she speaks, her voice is all Brooklyn and Queens
and so sweetly endeared my hungry ear feasts.
She doesn't eat much, but her belly seems
supple enough. Her breasts, what I've seen
of them when she bends, pale and quick as minnows.
I wonder what her nipples most resemble.
Her hips are wide, salty as the ocean
where she thrills to swim, sharp hips I'm dying
to float upon, or sink under and drown in.
Her belly button is pierced deep and sports
a stainless steel ring. She has three tattoos
and fingernails torn ragged enough to scratch

my back bloody in ecstasy. We don't have
long enough to live. I've longed to tuck her
dark hair back behind her ear, then lick
her there, on that little bone at the base
of her skull. Her lips? Full and chapped. I want
to bite them. I've dreamed her tongue inside me,
dreamed our teeth clicking together in the dark
room our mouths make. Her teeth are bad.
Yes, bad like mine.

HER HUSBAND

A moody guy, he broods all day.
Sits around in his crown of nettles and flame,

listening to death metal music,
thrashing along with his own guitar's shriek in headphones.

Staring down into that vast abyss he owns.
Where all the dead still live.

I just don't know what to do with him, she says.
His words to her ring harsh enough to make her cringe.

But he never means it.
Always begs forgiveness with a bouquet of black orchids.

She spends too much time with me.
He doesn't like that.

When the moon hands of midnight stand together,
she hugs me, then vanishes like ice fog in wind.

All night they make love
while the wind-torn world freezes solid white above them.

IN HER FOREST

Mosquitoes love her. Wherever
she walks in the world they swarm
a starving cloud around her, snared

in her wild hair like living confetti.
Somehow she suffers their little loves,
scratches the bites until she bleeds,

but never slaps the bugs silly or dead.
She must taste really good. Really good.
Sometimes they suck too much blood

and explode before they can withdraw
their pointy proboscises from her sweet flesh,
from their blood feast. When she pees

out in her forest, out among her spruce trees
they flock for her butt with a happy whine
of tiny wings. Once I saw her transform

into a swallow and, swooping like no
bird ever before through that evening's air,
snatch up every last one of those mosquitoes.

MIRABEL

i. Then

And now she's coming out
from her mother's body all
bloody and blue, mother heaving
daughter out blue and bloody

and then time bends so
forever happens in a second
while whole weeks disappear
like late spring snow under

longer sun, each month slumping
into itself until the trees have leaves
again. Her azure eyes open
and she gazes up at me, bloody

and trapped in time. Who are you, strange
creature? she wonders, and sleeps
on my arm those melting days. She grows.
And so does my arm to hold her steady.

Her sleep, when she sleeps, is perfect.
She sleeps the spring sprawled there
on my arm and time bends with her
dreaming until summer comes

and the garden blooms. She stretches
to pull new peas from the vine.

Me? I'm learning to crawl again,
hands and knees sinking into loam

since she blooms out, becoming
human from the belly first, her feet
still frightening blue, my feet in miniature,
her mother torn and bleeding

and her still bloody on mother's belly
already reaching toward the nipple
where milk is already ready
for her to drink to grow. I see she

is woman too, daughter, mother
torn and bleeding. Time bends, her
wet hair still blooming out until
I don't know who is being born.

ii. September

Born boreal, late April, she never
knew the sun might set. Now
it's fall already and the birch

leaves she loves have turned to fire
she watches flicker to the ground.
Now there is night and each night

longer until cold flows down from the hills
and soon the snow will come. Winter's
coming. She holds tight and we try

to keep warm before the cold kills us all.
She's never seen snow, but I'm pretty sure
she'll love that too: dry zero on her cheeks

when snow blinds windless nights and a new
silver ball rises through green flame. She stretches
her arms up to it, whispers, *Goodnight, Moon.*

iii. Raspberries

She has her bucket, but she won't need it.
The thing about raspberries, she says, is
you have to pick them fast and eat them up.

She doesn't care that berryless winter's coming,
but at our backs this close to the highway I hear
time's eighteen-wheeled chariots roaring near.

In front of us, the cliff. Careful, I keep
saying. Keep your balance. It's beautiful,
she says, meaning the berry in her hand,

the berry in her mouth, the canes loaded
with berries, the field, late July, sky and clouds
and fireweed blooming near the end, the bog

below us loaded with blueberries, salmon berries,
cranberries, crowberries, moss and spruce.
Meaning the alder thicket we'll wade later

to get there. Meaning everything all caught
on the lopsided wheel of seed and sudden
death. Raspberries taste, she says, like sun.

iv. New House on Narrowview Lane

Turn right off Breeze and you're practically here.
We're the fifth driveway on the left, past
three dog yards, past the bus where we suspect
they're cooking meth, past the collector of dead
cars and the big log cabin next to him.
You'll know it's the driveway when you see
the big No Trespassing sign we decided
to leave up. It's an A-frame with a green
metal roof. They found the woman who lived
here before, huddled with her eleven dogs
in the middle of winter, out of wood,
out of water, out of her mind with the long
night, or sorrow for the man who'd up
and left her here like this. They hauled her off,
the people who sold it to us said. You wouldn't
believe it's the same place. First week here we had
wolves in the hills and an owl on the roof.
Now October's coming on and all afternoon
chainsaws whine through birch. The leaves long
gone, and today wind bends the spruce double.
Geese and cranes long gone too, but the owl will
winter here, and today down by the river
we saw a falcon stoop and take a ruffed grouse.
About half the folks on our road have running
water. We do, but it's been some years since
we did, and Mirabel sure loves her new bathtub.
There's a garden spot in front, forest in back,
high bush cranberries, raspberries, amanita
muscaria everywhere. What else? It's moose
season and rifle shots mean somebody's meat.

Plenty of bear sign not far from the house.
You'll see when you get here. We're close to
North Pole, closer to Two Rivers and mountains
hover above a sea of mist at the end of the road
these crystal fall mornings. The bears are fat
and sleepy this time of year, but they haven't
denned up yet. We all have guns on Narrowview Lane,
and we keep them loaded. What else can I tell you?
Come on up for a visit as soon as you can.

v. Big Plan

Let's do it. I's ready. Let's go downstairs.
I's hungry. Can we cook up some eggs and catsup?
That's what I want. Can I have some butter?
Can we feed the fish? Let's go give
the chickens a snack and look for eggs.
That sounds like a good idea. Can we kill a chicken?
I's hungry. What'd you do? Is it dead? Look at it bleed!
Can I pluck it? Do chickens' insides have names?
Do we have insides like chickens?
Can you take my insides out so I can see?
I like breast the best. Can we cook it up?
I's hungry. Let's start the fire. Chicken's good.
You want to draw with me? That would be a good idea.
Want to build a train? Whoa! Look at it go!
Let's go upstairs and read a book.
Then we can read another one book.
Then we can close our eyes and go to sleep.
That would be a good idea.

vi. Meeting Death

Silly, silly flies, she says,
shooing them away from
our friend Harry's furry

corpse. Harry, who was
bright-eyed and nibbling
a carrot not two hours ago

now stiff and on his side,
his two yellowed front teeth
protruding like a bad comic's.

Death is a bad comic,
the timing always off,
too soon, too soon. Harry

was an old Guinea Pig,
devourer of lettuce, toe licker,
prodigious pooper. Too soon.

We'll dig him a new house,
she says. A new house
in the woods behind our new

house in the woods. She will
lift him (*I'm being very gentle*)
then plunk him in. She has

known Harry all her life
and a quarter of his. *Will
you die too,* she'll ask me

when she wakes in the middle
of the night. I go for the shovel
and weep. When I come back

she's kneeling beside his cage,
keeping off the flies. *I know
Harry,* she says, *I know.*

vii. Thoughts on the Subject

1. If I like the gun and the chainsaw I'd better get
used to them because they is very loud.
And I want to shoot a moose and eat it. That's true.

2. If we had the shotgun right now we could shoot
that grouse. We could.

3. If I took the insides out of the Kitty,
if I took the skin off the Kitty,
I could see what the Kitty has inside.
What does the Kitty have inside?
The same stuff as us?
But then the Kitty would be dead
and we would have no Kitty.

4. I'm gonna cut off your head
with my scissors and it will hurt
very much and you will bleed
and then you'll die and then I won't
have a daddy and I'll be very sad.

5. Will we be dead someday?
When we are dead will all our blood run out?
We have to take very good care of me
or I could die. I could.

KENNICOTT

When words turned bitter
on my tongue, before you

had words, but plenty of cries
to say you were bitter too,

we followed the creek up
past the abandoned copper

mine to the glacier, past tourists
and shops to the receding

glacier on a hot August day,
smaller than it was last year,

smaller than it was in May.
Because the sun was a fire

in our eyes, and sleep seemed
far away, we watched Cessnas

flying flightseers overhead.
Could they see us waving up

from the moraine? Because sleep
wouldn't stop for us and the light

was light all night we stumbled back
down to the creek to hear many-voiced

waters rolling boulders closer,
closer to the sea. How else to say it?

The only reason I exist is
because you love me.